FOOD JOKES

Compiled by Pam Rosenberg • Illustrated by Mernie Gallagher-Cole

The Child's World

Published by The Child's World®
1980 Lookout Drive
Mankato, MN 56003-1705
800-599-READ
www.childsworld.com

The Child's World®: Mary Berendes, Publishing Director
Editorial Directions, Inc.: E. Russell Primm, Editorial
Director; Lucia Raatma, Copyeditor and Proofreader;
Jennifer Zeiger and Joshua Gregory, Editorial Assistants
The Design Lab: Design and production

Library of Congress Cataloging-in-Publication Data
Food jokes / compiled by Pam Rosenberg ;
illustrated by Mernie Gallagher-Cole.
       p. cm.
   ISBN 978-1-60253-518-3 (library bound : alk. paper)
   1. Food—Juvenile humor. I. Rosenberg, Pam.
   II. Gallagher-Cole, Mernie. III. Title.
   PN6231.F66F66 2010
   818'.6020803559—dc22   2010002049

Printed in the United States of America
Mankato, Minnesota
July 2010
F11538

ABOUT THE AUTHOR

Pam Rosenberg is the author of more than 50 books for children. She lives near Chicago, Illinois, with her husband and two children.

ABOUT THE ILLUSTRATOR

Mernie Gallagher-Cole lives in Pennsylvania with her husband and two children. She has illustrated many children's books for The Child's World®.

TABLE OF CONTENTS

4 Bread and Grain Jokes

5 Dairy Jokes

7 Fruit and Vegetable Jokes

14 Sweet and Snack Jokes

16 Meat and Fish Jokes

21 Condiment Jokes

22 More Food Jokes

BREAD AND GRAIN JOKES

Q: Why was the stale loaf of bread arrested?
A: It tried to get fresh.

Q: Did you hear the joke about the oatmeal?
A: It's a lot of mush.

Q: Why did the lazy man want a job in the bakery?
A: So he could loaf around.

Q: What's the difference between the sun and a loaf of bread?

A: The sun rises in the east, and the bread rises from yeast.

....

DANIEL: Why is this bread full of holes?

SCHOOL COOK: Because it's whole wheat bread.

....

CITY KID: Do you like raisin bread?

FARMER: Don't know. Never raised any.

DAIRY JOKES

Q: What do cows give after an earthquake?

A: Milk shakes.

....

Q: What do dogs put on their pizza?

A: Mutts-arella cheese.

....

Q: What did the egg say to the farmer?

A: "I'm too young to fry!"

Q: Why did the egg go to the doctor?
A: It was cracking up.

Q: How do you make a cream puff?
A: Chase it around the kitchen.

Q: Why did the boy throw butter out the window?
A: He wanted to see a butterfly.

Q: What do you get from a pampered cow?
A: Spoiled milk.

Q: Which hand should you use to butter a roll?
A: Neither. You use a butter knife.

Q: What do outlaws eat with their milk?
A: Crookies.

Q: What do you get when you cross a camera with a mouse?
A: Cheese!

Q: How do you fix a cracked pumpkin?

A: With a pumpkin patch.

Q: What has ears but can't hear anything?

A: A cornfield.

Q: What vegetable is dangerous to have on a boat?

A: A leek.

Q: How do you make a strawberry shake?

A: Take it to a scary movie.

Q: What did the baby corn say to the mama corn?

A: "Where's Pop Corn?"

Q: Why did the people like to dance to the vegetable band?

A: Because it had a good beet.

Q: What did one banana sitting in the sun say to the other banana sitting in the sun?

A: "I don't know about you, but I'm starting to peel."

Q: What do you get when two peas fight?

A: Black-eyed peas.

Q: Why was the baby strawberry crying?

A: Because its mother was in a jam.

Q: What happens when 3,000 blueberries all try to go through the door at the same time?

A: Blueberry jam.

KNOCK, KNOCK.

Who's there?

Lettuce.

Lettuce who?

Lettuce in and you'll find out!

Q: What is green and sings?
A: Elvis Parsely

SCHOOL COOK: Eat your vegetables. Green things are good for you.

ANNA: Okay. Then I'll have some pistachio ice cream.

Q: What kind of room can you eat?
A: A mush-room.

....

Q: Why did the banana go to the doctor?
A: It wasn't peeling well.

....

Q: What is brown and hairy and wears sunglasses?
A: A coconut on its summer vacation.

....

Q: What's bright orange and sounds like a parrot?
A: A carrot.

....

Q: How do you fix a broken tomato?
A: With tomato paste.

....

Q: When do you go at red and stop at green?
A: When you're eating a watermelon.

....

Q: If a carrot and a cabbage ran a race, who would win?
A: The cabbage, because it's a head.

Q: Why couldn't the magician tell his magic secrets in the garden?

A: Because the corn has ears and the potatoes have eyes.

....

Q: Why did the man stare at the can of orange juice?

A: It said "concentrate" on the label.

....

Q: Did you hear about the banana that snored?

A: He woke up the whole bunch.

....

Q: How do you know carrots are good for your eyes?

A: Because you never see rabbits wearing glasses.

....

Q: Why couldn't the orange finish the race?

A: It ran out of juice.

....

Q: How many lemons grow on a lemon tree?

A: All of them.

Q: What was the nearsighted chicken doing in the farmer's garden?
A: She was sitting on an eggplant.

Q: Why were the orange and the apple all alone?
A: Because the banana split.

Q: If an apple a day keeps the doctor away, what does an onion a day do?
A: It keeps everybody away.

Q: What would you get if you crossed a sweet potato with a jazz musician?
A: Yam sessions.

SWEET AND SNACK JOKES

Q: Where do you go to learn how to make a banana split?
A: Sundae school.

Q: What's the best thing to eat in a bathtub?
A: Sponge cake.

....

Q: Why did the cookie go to the hospital?
A: It felt crumby.

....

Q: What do you call a bear with no teeth?
A: A gummy bear.

....

Q: What do you call a person who can drink soda and sing at the same time?
A: A pop singer.

....

Q: What do nuts sound like when they sneeze?
A: Cashew!

....

Q: Why did the student eat his homework?
A: Because his teacher told him it was a piece of cake.

MEAT AND FISH JOKES

Q: Why do chickens never play baseball?
A: Because they hit fowl balls.

Q: What do astronauts put on their sandwiches?
A: Launch meat.

Q: What kind of alarms do fast food restaurants have?
A: Burger alarms.

Q: What's the worst thing about being an octopus?

A: Washing your hands before dinner.

Q: What kind of food talks the most?

A: A talk-o.

CUSTOMER: What do you call this dish?

WAITER: Chicken surprise.

CUSTOMER: But I don't see any chicken in it.

WAITER: That's the surprise!

Q: What did one hot dog say to another?

A: "Hi, Frank!"

Q: How did the butcher introduce his wife?

A: "Meat Patty."

Q: What town in England makes terrible sandwiches?

A: Oldham.

Q: What do you get when you cross a cheetah with a hamburger?

A: Fast food.

....

CUSTOMER: Do you serve crabs here?

WAITER: Yep. We'll serve just about anybody!

....

Q: Did you hear about the fight in the fish shop last night?

A: Two fish got battered!

....

Q: What was the hamburger's favorite fairy tale?

A: Hansel and Gristle.

....

Q: Why do the hamburgers beat the hot dogs at every sport they play?

A: Because the hot dogs are the wurst.

....

Q: Where does a hot dog go when it gets good grades?

A: On the honor roll.

Q: Why did the fried chicken cross the road?
A: Because he saw a fork up ahead.

....

Q: Why did the skeleton visit the butcher?
A: Because he needed some spare ribs.

....

Q: What has bread on both sides and frightens easily?
A: A chicken sandwich.

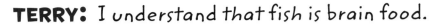

TERRY: I understand that fish is brain food.

BRAD: Yes, I eat it all the time.

TERRY: Well, there goes another scientific theory.

KNOCK, KNOCK.
Who's there?
Gorilla.
Gorilla who?
Gorilla me a
hamburger.
I'm hungry!

20

CONDIMENT JOKES

KNOCK, KNOCK.
Who's there?
Ketchup.
Ketchup who?
Ketchup and maybe
I'll tell you!

Q: Why was the mayonnaise late for the game?
A: Because it was dressing.

....

Q: What did the salt say to the pepper?
A: "Hey, what's shakin'?"

....

Q: Did you hear about the man who was so absentminded he poured ketchup on his shoelaces and tied knots in his spaghetti?

21

MORE FOOD JOKES

Q: What has four legs and flies?
A: A picnic table.

Q: What did the mother ghost tell the baby ghost when he ate too fast?
A: Stop goblin your food!

Q: Why is a chef mean?
A: Because he beats the eggs, mashes the potatoes, and whips the cream.

ANNA: I trained my dog not to beg at the table.

TONY: How did you do that?

ANNA: I let him taste my cooking.

Q: Why did the man have lunch at a bank?

A: He wanted a rich meal.

Q: What does a shark eat with peanut butter?

A: Jellyfish.

Q: What starts with T, ends with T, and is filled with T?

A: A teapot.

Q: What does a lion eat when he goes to a restaurant?

A: The waiter.

Q: What does the world's richest person like to make for dinner?

A: Reservations.

Q: What did one plate say to the other?
A: Dinner's on me.

Q: What do frogs drink at picnics?
A: Croak-a-cola.

Q: Why didn't the teddy bear eat his dinner?
A: Because he was stuffed.

Q: How do aliens drink their tea?
A: In flying saucers.

Q: What are two things you can't have for lunch?
A: Breakfast and dinner.

Q: What happened when the diver fell into a glass of root beer?
A: Nothing. It was a soft drink.